First Step in Phonics

Beginning
Consonants

Clue & Key

Contents

b · c

 Listen and chant. ◉ 02

bat **ball** **butter**

AB ✏ **Write the letters.**

bat **ball** **butter**

at **all** **utter**

Listen and chant. 🔘 03

cap   coat   cookie

 Write the letters.

cap   coat   cookie

ap   oat   ookie

a
b
c
d
e
f
g
h
i
j
k
l
m
n
o
p
q
r
s
t
u
v
w
x
y
z

5

Listen and color the pictures with the same beginning sounds. ◎ 04

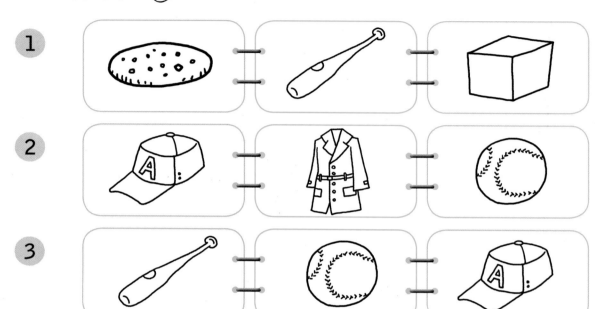

1

2

3

Circle and write.

1  (b) c

ball

2 b c

oat

3  b c

ookie

4 b c

utter

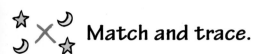
Match and trace.

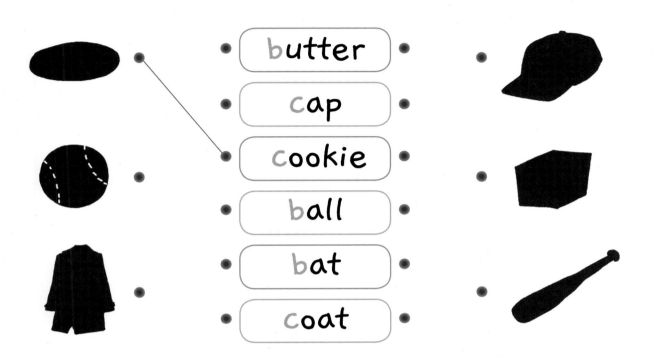

butter

cap

cookie

ball

bat

coat

Write the words.

cap   ball   butter   bat   coat   cookie

b

ball

c

cap

a
b
c
d
e
f
g
h
i
j
k
l
m
n
o
p
q
r
s
t
u
v
w
x
y
z

7

Phonics Story

 Listen and read aloud. 🔘 05~06

I want a ball.

I want a bat.

I want a cap.

Wow! I want cookies.

 Read the words. 🔘 07

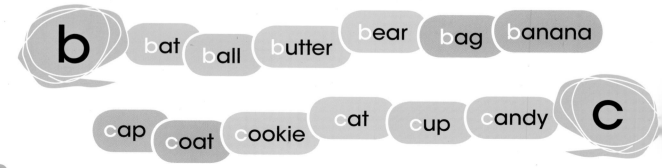

b bat ball butter bear bag banana

cap coat cookie cat cup candy **c**

Write the beginning letters.

1  c

2

Circle the words.

1  (bat) coat

2 ball cap

Listen and check if the words begin with the same sound. 08

1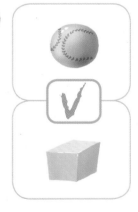

2

3

Listen and number. 09

1

Listen and chant. 🔘 10

dish   door   donut

 **Write the letters.**

dish   door   donut

ish   oor   onut

Listen and chant. ⊙ 11

fox   **frog**   **flower**

 Write the letters.

fox   **frog**   **flower**

ox   **rog**   **lower**

a
b
c
d
e
f
g
h
i
j
k
l
m
n
o
p
q
r
s
t
u
v
w
x
y
z

Listen and write the beginning sounds. 🔘 12

1

2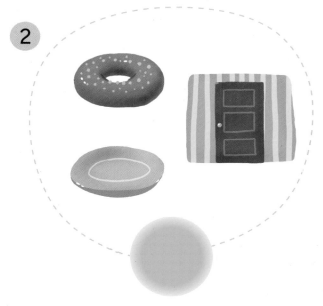

Circle and write.

1  d

f

ish

2  d

f

lower

3  d

f

rog

4  d

f

onut

Match and trace.

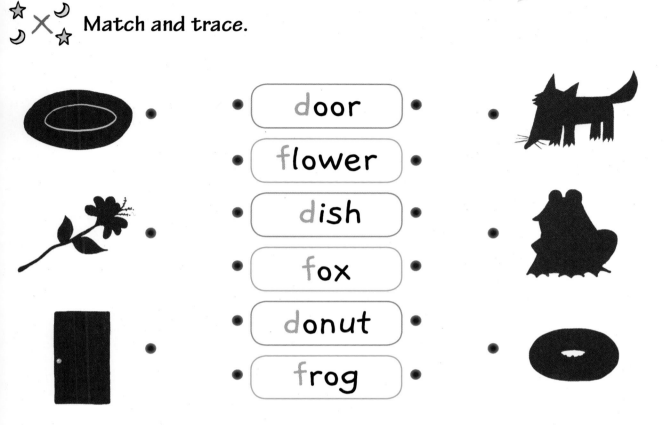

door	flower	dish
fox	donut	frog

Write the words.

donut dish fox door frog flower

d

f

a b c d e f g h i j k l m n o p q r s t u v w x y z

Phonics Story

 Listen and read aloud. 🔘 13~14

A dish is on the table.

A fork and fish are on the table.

Donuts are on the dish.

A flower is on the table.

 Read the words. 🔘 15

d   dish   door   donut   dog   desk   duck

fox   frog   flower   fish   fan   fork   f

Write the beginning letters.

1

2

Circle the words.

1

door

frog

2

fox

dish

Listen and check if the words begin with the same sound. ⊙ 16

1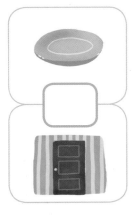

2

3

Listen and number. ⊙ 17

Listen and chant. ◎ 18

gift   **g**oat   **g**lass

 Write the letters.

gift   **g**oat   **g**lass

ift   oat   lass

Listen and chant. ◉ 19

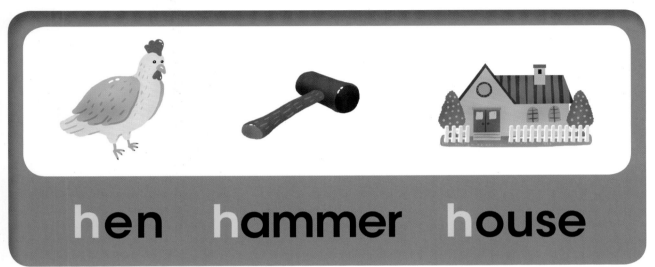

h en   h ammer   h ouse

 Write the letters.

h en   h ammer   h ouse

en   ammer   ouse

a
b
c
d
e
f
g
h
i
j
k
l
m
n
o
p
q
r
s
t
u
v
w
x
y
z

😊 ⊗ **Cross out the one that has a different beginning sound.** ⊙ 20

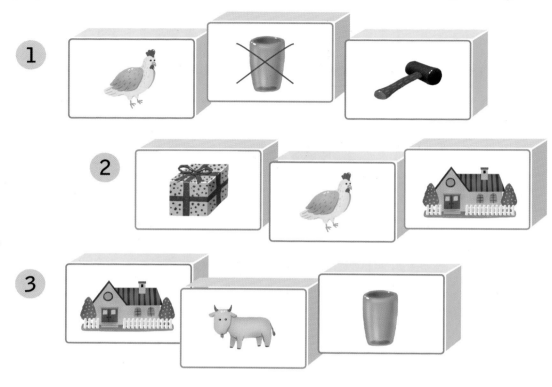

✏️ AB **Circle and write.**

1. g / h

ouse

2. g / h

en

3. g / h

lass

4. g / h

oat

Match and trace.

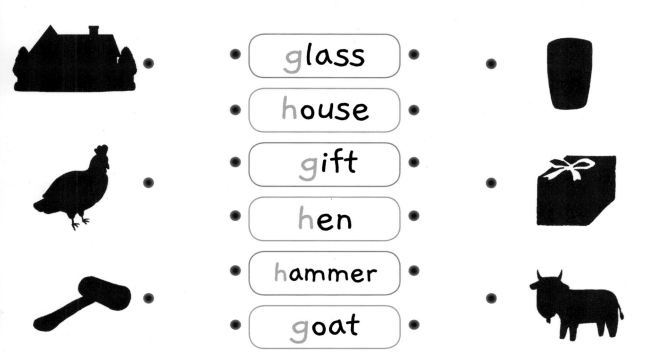

glass

house

gift

hen

hammer

goat

Write the words.

hammer   house   goat   glass   hen   gift

g

h

a
b
c
d
e
f
g
h
i
j
k
l
m
n
o
p
q
r
s
t
u
v
w
x
y
z

Phonics Story

 Listen and read aloud. 🔘 21-22

Give me a gift.

Thank you for the hen.

Thank you for the goat.

Please give me a hand.

 Read the words. 🔘 23

 **g**   gift   goat   glass   guitar   gorilla   girl

hen   hammer   house   hand   hat   hippo   **h**

Write the beginning letters.

1

2

Circle the words.

1   hen   gift

2   glass   house

Listen and check if the words begin with the same sound. 24

1

2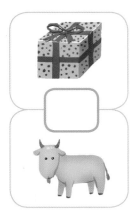

3

Listen and number. 25

Unit 04 j·k

 Listen and chant. 🎧 26

jar   jump   jungle

✏️ Write the letters.

jar   jump   jungle

ar   ump   ungle

Listen and chant. ⊙ 27

key **koala** **kangaroo**

 Write the letters.

key koala kangaroo

ey oala angaroo

a b c d e f g h i j **k** l m n o p q r s t u v w x y z

23

Listen and color the pictures with the same beginning sounds. ⊙ 28

1

2

3

Circle and write.

1

j

k

oala

2

j

k

ey

3

j

k

ungle

4

j

k

ar

Match and trace.

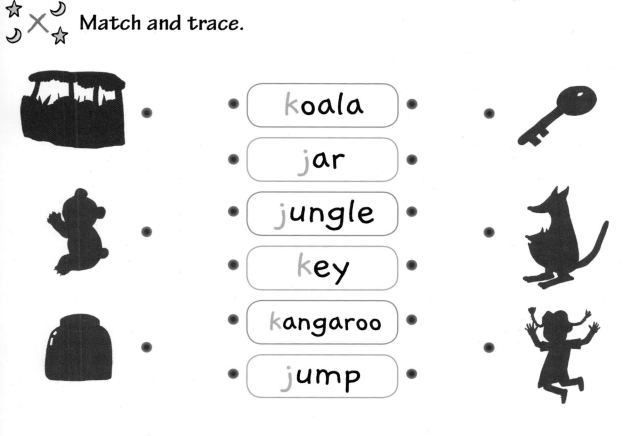

koala

jar

jungle

key

kangaroo

jump

Write the words.

jar   key   koala   jungle   kangaroo   jump

j

k

a
b
c
d
e
f
g
h
i
j
k
l
m
n
o
p
q
r
s
t
u
v
w
x
y
z

Listen and read aloud. 29~30

 Read the words. 31

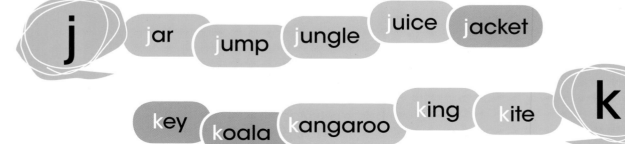

Write the beginning letters.

 1

2

Circle the words.

1   jar
jump

2   key
koala

Listen and check if the words begin with the same sound. 32

1

2

3

Listen and number. 33

27

l · m

 Listen and chant. 🔘 34

leg   **l**emon   **l**izard

 Write the letters.

leg   **l**emon   **l**izard

eg   emon   izard

Listen and chant. 35

moon **milk** **mirror**

 Write the letters.

moon milk mirror

oon ilk irror

a
b
c
d
e
f
g
h
i
j
k
l
m
n
o
p
q
r
s
t
u
v
w
x
y
z

Listen and write the beginning sounds. ◎ 36

1

2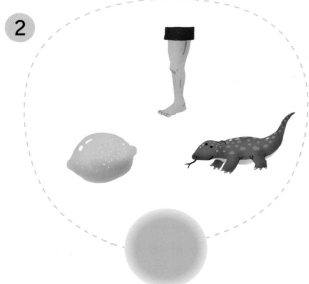

 Circle and write.

1 l
m

irror

2 l
m

emon

3  l
m

eg

4 l
m

ilk

Match and trace.

lemon

milk

mirror

leg

moon

lizard

Write the words.

lizard   lemon   moon   milk   leg   mirror

l

m

a
b
c
d
e
f
g
h
i
j
k
l
m
n
o
p
q
r
s
t
u
v
w
x
y
z

31

Phonics Story

 Listen and read aloud. 🔊 37~38

I see the moon.

I see the lemons.

I see the lizard.

It's me!

 Read the words. 🔊 39

l leg lemon lizard lion lamp

moon milk mirror monkey mouse **m**

Write the beginning letters.

1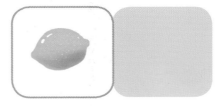

2

Circle the words.

1   lizard
         leg

2   moon
                        milk

Listen and check if the words begin with the same sound. 🔘 40

1

2

3

Listen and number. 🔘 41

REVIEW

 Listen and repeat. ◉ 42

b ··········

c ··········

d ··········

f ··········

g ··········

 Read the words quickly.

ball	cap	dish	gift	frog
fox	coat	bat	glass	donut
cookie	butter	flower	door	goat

Listen and repeat. 43

h · · · · · · · · · ·

j · · · · · · · · · ·

k · · · · · · · · · ·

l · · · · · · · · · ·

m · · · · · · · · · ·

 Read the words quickly.

| koala | mirror | jar | house | leg |

| jungle | hen | lizard | milk | hammer |

| key | lemon | moon | jump | kangaroo |

AB 🖊 **Listen and write.** 💿 44

1

b

2

3

4

5

6

7

8

🖊 **Circle.**

1

b h (m)

2

j k l

3

h l m

4

d f h

5

d h l

6

b f g

7

c f h

8

f g h

9

b c d

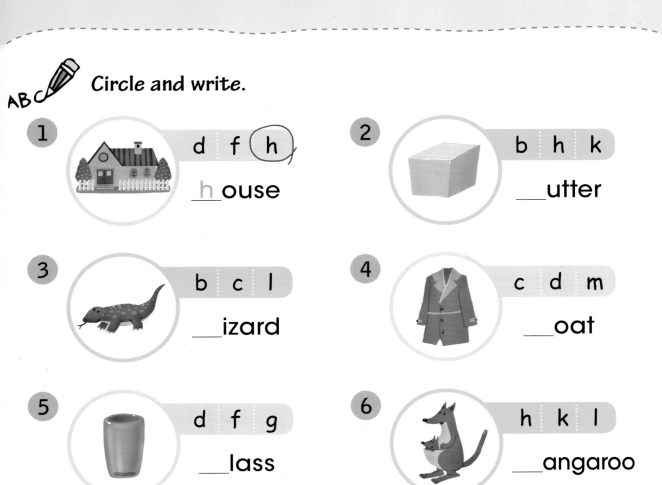

Circle and write.

1. d f (h)

   __h__ ouse

2. b h k

   ___utter

3. b c l

   ___izard

4. c d m

   ___oat

5. d f g

   ___lass

6. h k l

   ___angaroo

Match and write.

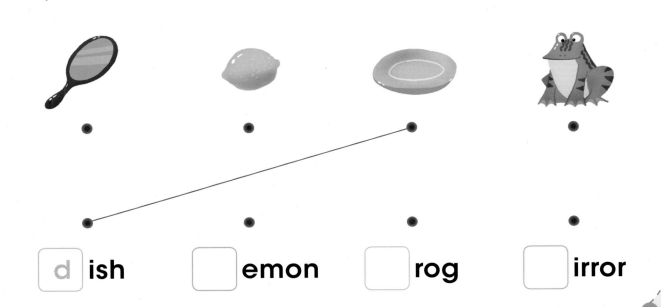

| d | ish | | emon | | rog | | irror |

Follow the correct letters for the pictures.

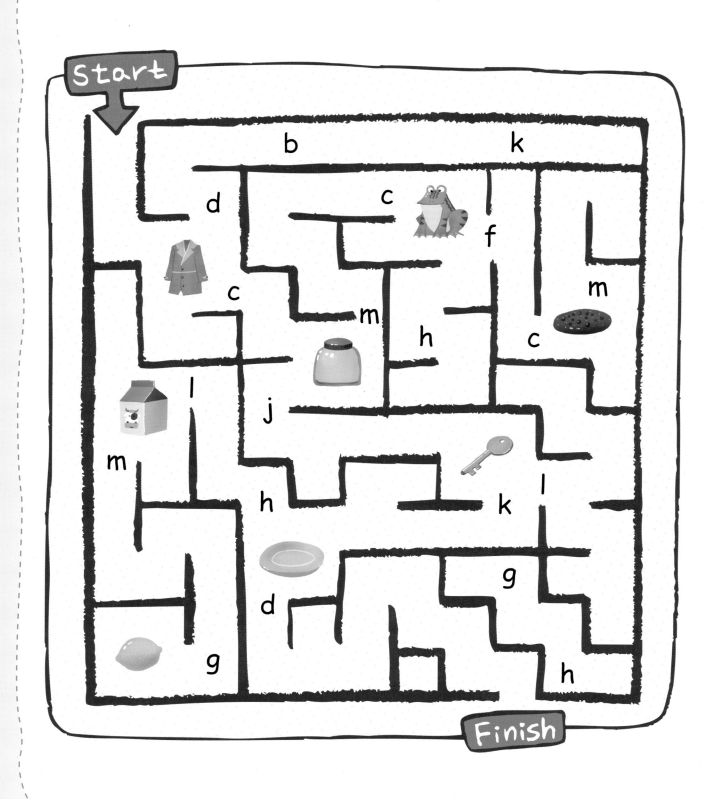

Circle three pictures that begin with the same sound.

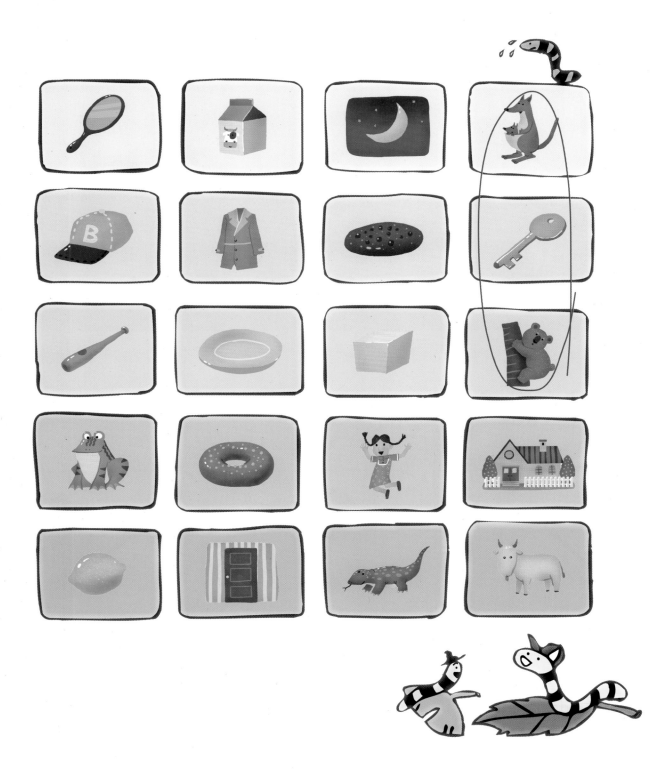

Unit 06 n · p

🎤 **Listen and chant.** 💿 45

net   nine   nest

✏️ **Write the letters.**

net   nine   nest

et   ine   est

Listen and chant. 🔘 46

piano   pencil   penguin

 Write the letters.

piano   **p**encil   **p**enguin

iano   encil   enguin

a b c d e f g h i j k l m n o p q r s t u v w x y z

😊 ❌ **Cross out the one that has a different beginning sound.** 💿 47

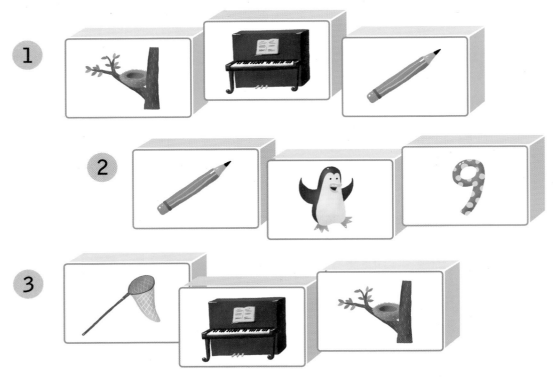

ABC✏️ **Circle and write.**

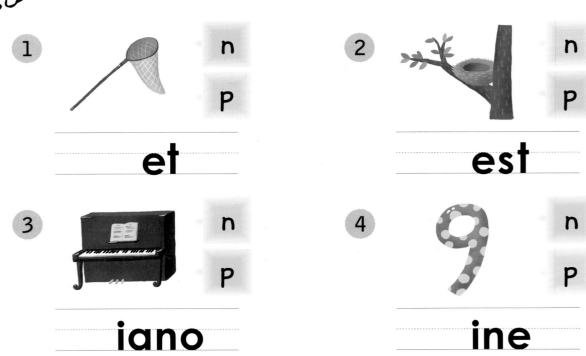

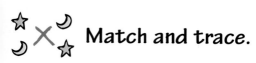 **Match and trace.**

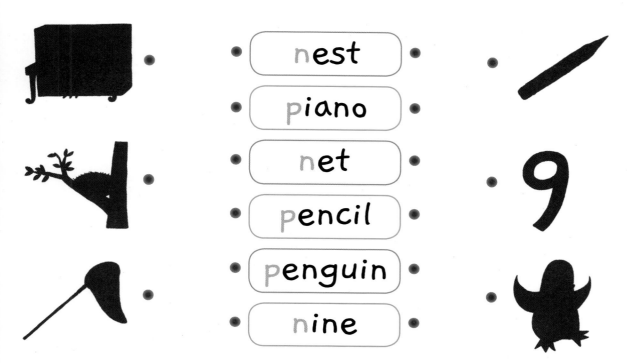

nest

piano

net

pencil

penguin

nine

AB ✏ **Write the words.**

pencil   penguin   net   piano   nine   nest

n

P

a
b
c
d
e
f
g
h
i
j
k
l
m
n
o
p
q
r
s
t
u
v
w
x
y
z

Listen and read aloud. 48~49

Look at the nine penguins.

Look at the nine pianos.

Look at the nine nests.

They are my pencils.

 Read the words. 50

n net nine nest nose neck

piano pencil penguin pig panda **p**

Write the beginning letters.

1

2

Circle the words.

1

nine

nest

2

pencil

net

Listen and check if the words begin with the same sound. 🔘 51

1

2

3

Listen and number. 🔘 52

Listen and chant. 🔊 53

quiz   quiet   question

 **Write the letters.**

quiz   quiet   question

uiz   uiet   uestion

Listen and chant. ◎ 54

red **roof** **rainbow**

 Write the letters.

red roof rainbow

ed oof ainbow

a
b
c
d
e
f
g
h
i
j
k
l
m
n
o
p
q
r
s
t
u
v
w
x
y
z

47

Listen and circle the pictures with the same beginning sounds. ◎ 55

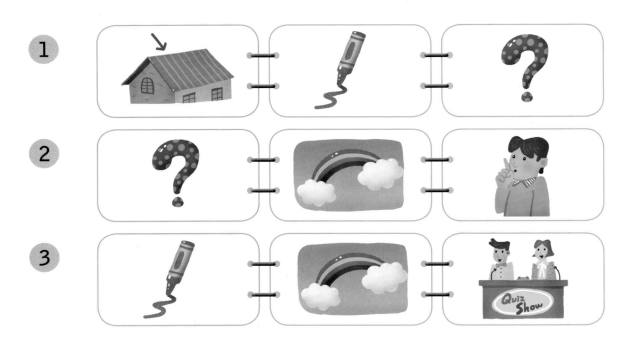

 Circle and write.

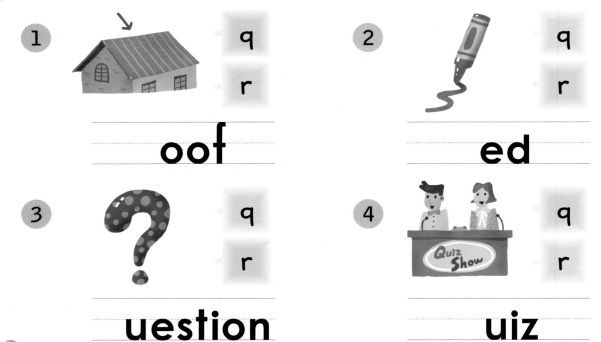

Match and trace.

roof

question

rainbow

quiz

quiet

red

Write the words.

rainbow roof question quiz red quiet

q

r

a
b
c
d
e
f
g
h
i
j
k
l
m
n
o
p
q
r
s
t
u
v
w
x
y
z

Phonics Story

 Listen and read aloud. ⊙ 56~57

All are red here.

Red robot and red quilt.

That is a red roof.

Look! That is a red rainbow!

 Read the words. ⊙ 58

q   quiz   quiet   question   queen   quilt

red   roof   rainbow   rabbit   robot   r

50

Write the beginning letters.

1

2

Circle the words.

1  quiet
roof

2   question
rainbow

Listen and check if the words begin with the same sound. 59

1

2

3

Listen and number. 60

 Listen and chant. 🔘 61

sun **sky** **sock**

 Write the letters.

sun   sky   sock

un   ky   ock

Listen and chant. 62

tent   tiger   turtle

 Write the letters.

tent   tiger   turtle

ent   iger   urtle

Listen and write the beginning sounds. ◉ 63

1
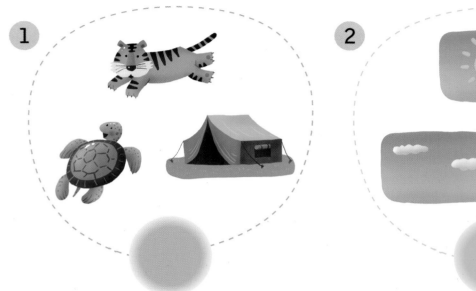

2
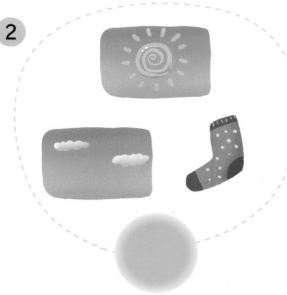

 Circle and write.

1

s
t

ock

2

s
t

urtle

3
s
t

ky

4

s
t

iger

Match and trace.

tiger

sky

turtle

sock

tent

sun

Write the words.

sky   tiger   tent   sun   turtle   sock

s

t

a
b
c
d
e
f
g
h
i
j
k
l
m
n
o
p
q
r
s
t
u
v
w
x
y
z

Phonics Story

 Listen and read aloud. 64~65

A turtle is in the sea.

The sun is in the sky.

The moon and stars are in the sky.

How beautiful!

 Read the words. 66

S

sun sky sock seven star

tent tiger turtle tomato table

Write the beginning letters.

1

2

Circle the words.

1

turtle

tent

2

sky

sun

Listen and check if the words begin with the same sound. 67

1

2

3

Listen and number. 68

🎤 Listen and chant. 💿 69

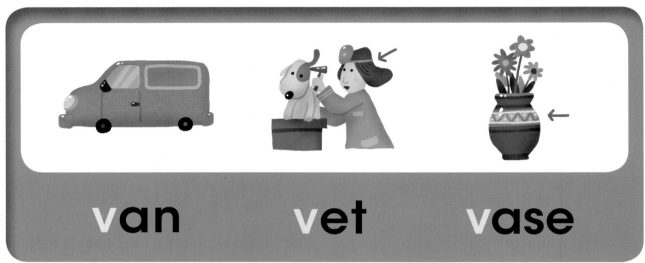

van   vet   vase

✏️ Write the letters.

van   vet   vase

an   et   ase

Listen and chant. 🔘 70

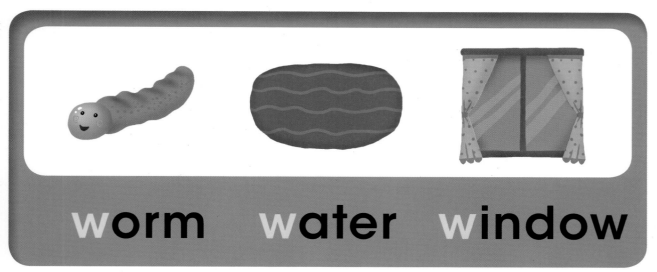

worm   water   window

 Write the letters.

   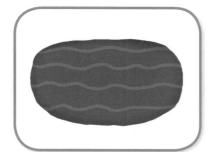   

worm   water   window

orm   ater   indow

a
b
c
d
e
f
g
h
i
j
k
l
m
n
o
p
q
r
s
t
u
v
w
x
y
z

☺ ⊗ **Cross out the one that has a different beginning sound.** ⊙ 71

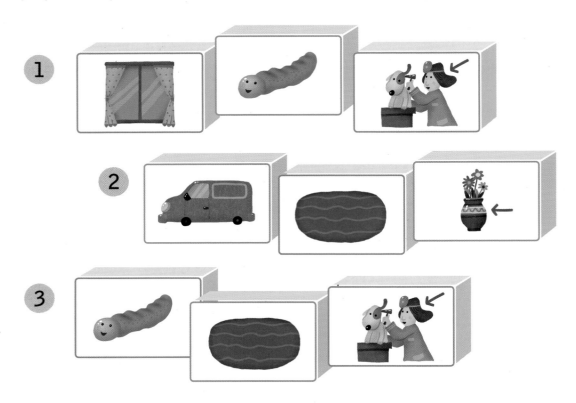

1

2

3

AB✏ **Circle and write.**

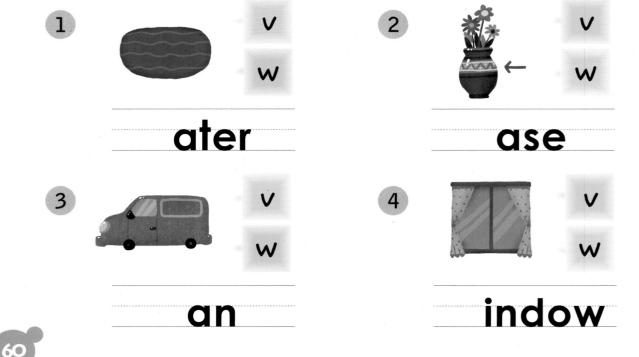

1   v
    w

ater

2   v
    w

ase

3   v
    w

an

4   v
    w

indow

⭐✖🌙 **Match and trace.**

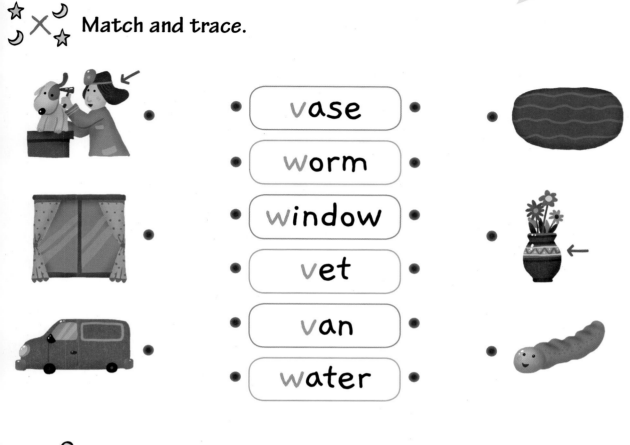

vase

worm

window

vet

van

water

ABC✏️ **Write the words.**

vet   window   vase   worm   water   van

V

W

a b c d e f g h i j k l m n o p q r s t u **v** **w** x y z

Phonics Story

Listen and read aloud. 72-73

 Read the words. 74

V van vet vase violin vest

worm water window watch wolf W

Write the beginning letters.

1

2

Circle the words.

1
vet
water

2
worm
vase

Listen and check if the words begin with the same sound. 75

1

2

3

Listen and number. 76

Unit 10

y · z

Listen and chant. ◎ 77

yak **yawn** **yellow**

Write the letters.

| **y**ak | **y**awn | **y**ellow |
| ak | awn | ellow |

Listen and chant. ◎ 78

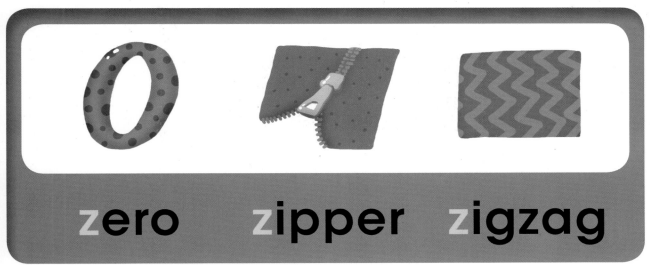

zero   zipper   zigzag

 Write the letters.

zero   zipper   zigzag

ero   ipper   igzag

Listen and color the pictures with the same beginning sounds. 🔘 79

1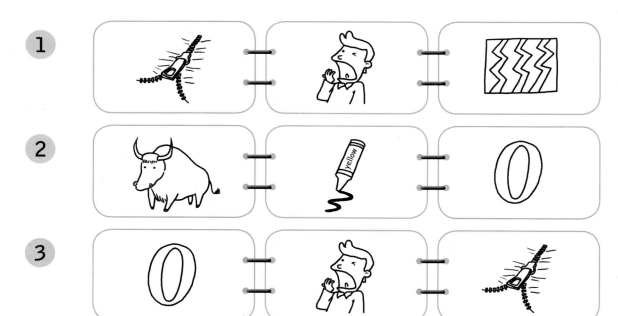

2

3

AB **Circle and write.**

1  y z

__ak__

2  y z

__igzag__

3   y z

__awn__

4   y z

__ellow__

Match and trace.

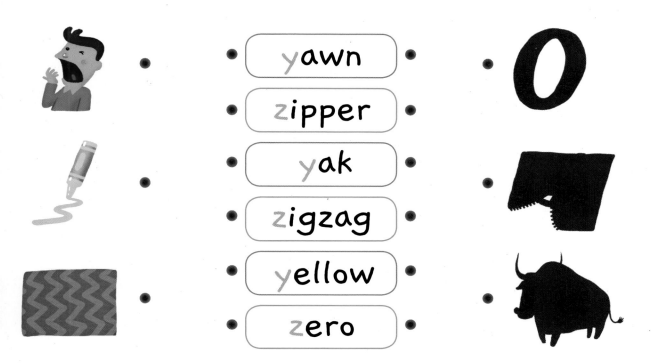

yawn

zipper

yak

zigzag

yellow

zero

Write the words.

zipper yak yellow zigzag yawn zero

y

z

a
b
c
d
e
f
g
h
i
j
k
l
m
n
o
p
q
r
s
t
u
v
w
x
y
z

Listen and read aloud. 80-81

 Read the words. 82

y   yak yawn yellow yacht yo-yo

zero zipper zigzag zebra zoo Z

Write the beginning letters.

1

2

Circle the words.

1

yak

yawn

2

zipper

zigzag

Listen and check if the words begin with the same sound. 83

1

2

3

Listen and number. ⊙ 84

REVIEW

 Listen and repeat. 🔘 85

n ·········

p ·········

q ·········

r ·········

s ·········

 Read the words quickly.

red	quiz	sock	net	penguin
nest	roof	sun	quiet	rainbow
sky	piano	nine	pencil	question

🎧 Listen and repeat. 💿 86

t ··········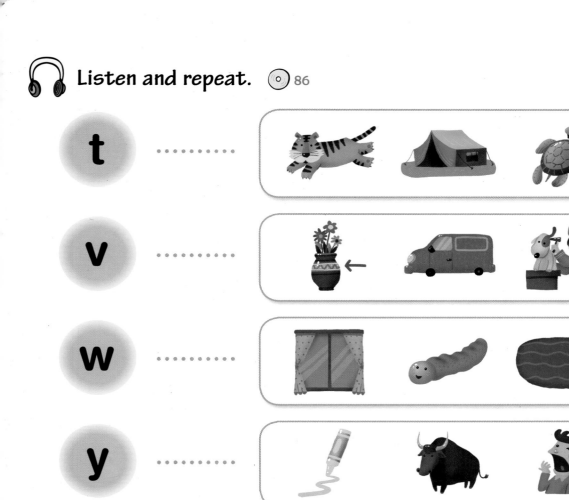

v ··········

w ··········

y ··········

z ··········

👄 Read the words quickly.

van	water	vase	tiger	yellow
yak	zipper	tent	worm	zigzag
vet	yawn	turtle	zero	window

AB ✏️ **Listen and write.** 🔘 87

1
_____

2
_____

3
_____

4
_____

5
_____

6
_____

7
_____

8
_____

✏️ **Circle.**

1

(n)   s   t

2

p   q   v

3

n   p   r

4

n   s   z

5

m   v   w

6

q   t   w

7

q   r   y

8

r   s   z

9

t   v   w

Circle and write.

1 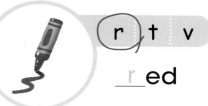 (r) t v

___r_ ed

2  n p y

___enguin

3  s t w

___urtle

4  n s z

___igzag

5  q v w

___uiz

6  n y z

___awn

 Match and write.

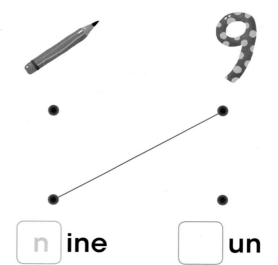  

| n | ine | | un | | et | | encil |

Follow the correct letters for the pictures.

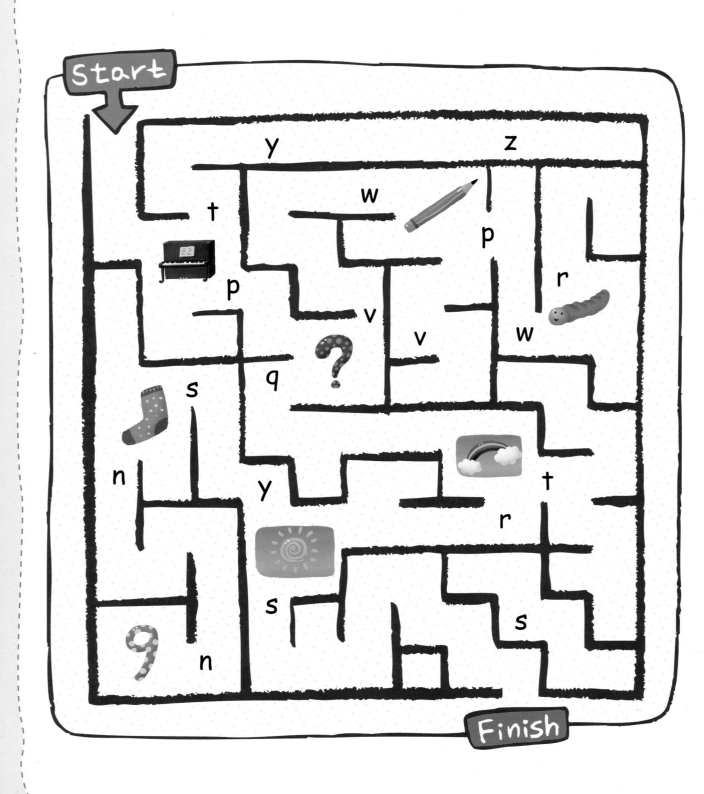

Circle three pictures that begin with the same sound.

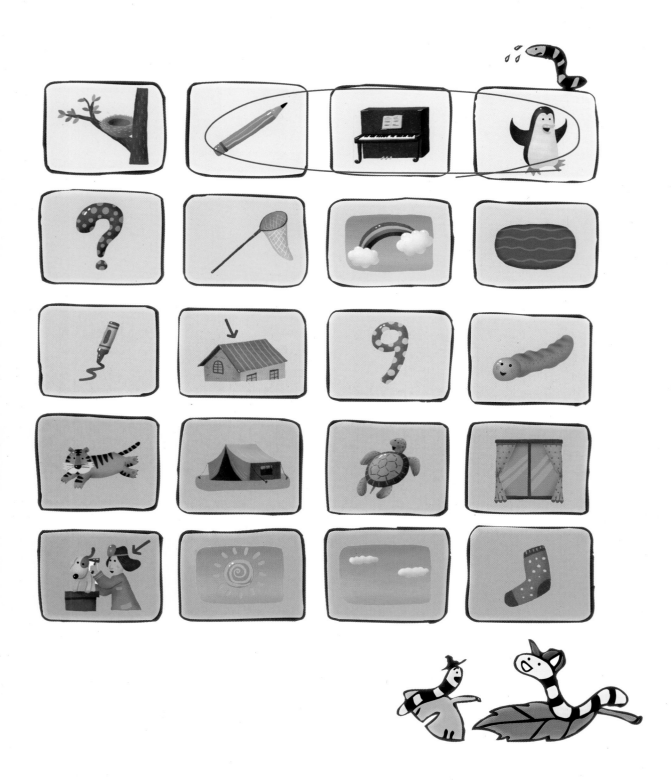

Word Review

 Read and write the words.

 bat

 ball

 butter

 cap

 coat

 cookie

 dish

 door

 donut

 fox

 frog

 flower

 gift

 goat

glass

hen

hammer

house

jar

jump

jungle

key

koala

kangaroo

leg

lemon

lizard

moon

milk

mirror

Read and write the words.

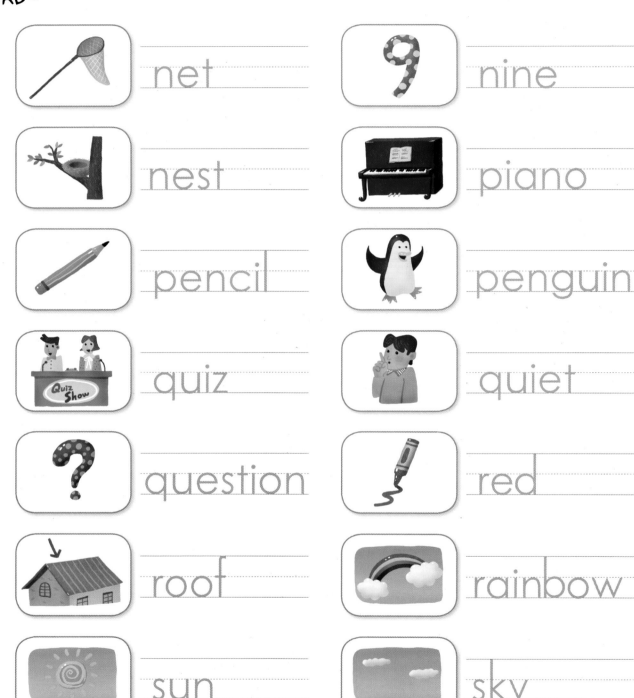

net

nine

nest

piano

pencil

penguin

quiz

quiet

question

red

roof

rainbow

sun

sky

 sock

 tent

 tiger

 turtle

 van

 vet

 vase

 worm

 water

 window

 yak

 yawn

 yellow

 zero

 zipper

 zigzag

Glossary

Unit 01

bat
ball
butter
cap
coat
cookie

Unit 02

dish
door
donut
fox
frog
flower

Unit 03

gift
goat
glass
hen
hammer
house

Unit 04

jar
jump

jungle
key
koala
kangaroo

Unit 05

leg
lemon
lizard
moon
milk
mirror

Unit 06

net
nine
nest
piano
pencil
penguin

Unit 07

quiz
quiet
question
red
roof
rainbow

Unit 08

sun
sky
sock
tent
tiger
turtle

Unit 09

van
vet
vase
worm
water
window

Unit 10

yak
yawn
yellow
zero
zipper
zigzag

First Step in Phonics

Workbook

AceME R&D Center

2

Beginning Consonants

Clue & Key

Contents

Unit 01   b · c

ABC ✏ **Say and write.**

bat

bat

ball

ball

butter

butter

cap

cap

coat

coat

cookie

cookie

Circle.

1
   (b) | c

2
   b | c

3
   b | c

4
   b | c

5
   b | c

6
   b | c

Circle.

1 cookie

2 ball

3 coat

4 bat

☆✕☽ **Match and trace.**

1  • • ball

2  • • cap

3  • • butter

4 • • cookie

ABC✏ **Read and write.**

I want a ball.
I want a ball.

I want a bat.

I want a cap.

Wow! I want cookies.

d · f

ABC Say and write.

dish

door

donut

dish

door

donut

fox

frog

flower

fox

frog

flower

 Match.

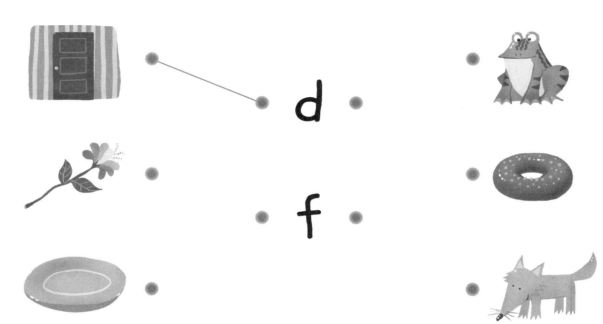

d

f

✏️ Circle.

1 door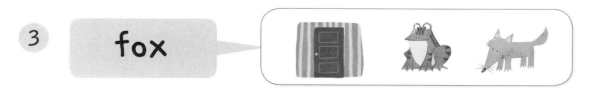

2 flower

3 fox

4 dish

☾✕☆ **Match and trace.**

1  •   • frog

2 •   • dish

3  •   • flower

4 •   • donut

ᴀʙᴄ✐ **Read and write.**

 A dish is on the table.

 A fork and fish are on the table.

 Donuts are on the dish.

 A flower is on the table.

7

ABC 🖊 **Say and write.**

gift

goat

glass

gift

goat

glass

hen

hammer

house

hen

hammer

house

✐ Circle.

1
(g | h)

2
(g | h)

3
(g | h)

4
(g | h)

5
(g | h)

6
(g | h)

✐ Circle.

1 **glass**

2 **hen**

3 **goat**

4 **hammer**

Match and trace.

1 •   • house

2 •   • gift

3  •   • hen

4 •   • goat

AB✏ **Read and write.**

 Give me a gift.

 Thank you for the hen.

 Thank you for the goat.

 Please give me a hand.

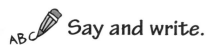

Unit 04 j·k

ABC 🖊 **Say and write.**

jar

jar

jump

jump

jungle

jungle

key

key

koala

koala

kangaroo

kangaroo

11

 Match.

 j

 k

 Circle.

1 jar

2 key

3 kangaroo

4 jungle

12

 Match and trace.

1 • • key

2 • • jar

3 • • koala

4 • • jump

Read and write.

 Draw a kangaroo.

 Draw a koala.

 I am drawing a jungle.

 Oh, they are in the jungle.

13

l · m

ABC Say and write.

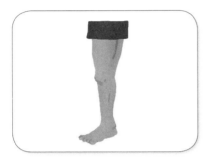
leg

leg

lemon

lemon

lizard

lizard

moon

moon

milk

milk

mirror

mirror

✏️ Circle.

1  (l | m)

2 (l | m)

3 (l | m)

4 (l | m)

5 (l | m)

6 (l | m)

✏️ Circle.

1 milk

2 lizard

3 lemon

4 mirror

15

 Match and trace.

1  ● ● leg

2  ● ● moon

3 ● ● milk

4 ● ● lizard

ABC✎ Read and write.

 I see the moon.

 I see the lemons.

 I see the lizard.

 It's me!

n·p

 Say and write.

net

net

nine

nine

nest

nest

piano

piano

pencil

pencil

penguin

penguin

 Match.

   •   •

        • n •

   •

        • P •

   •   •

 Circle.

1   piano

2   net

3   nest

4   pencil

⭐✖ **Match and write.**

1 ● ● penguin

2 ● ● nine

3 ● ● pencil

4 ● ● nest

ABC✏ **Read and write.**

 Look at the nine penguins.

 Look at the nine pianos.

 Look at the nine nests.

 They are my pencils.

 **Say and write.**

quiz

quiz

quiet

quiet

question

question

red

red

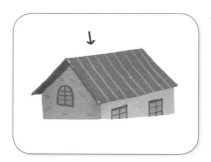

roof

roof

rainbow

rainbow

✏️ Circle.

1  q | r

2  q | r

3  q | r

4 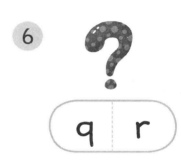 q | r

5 q | r

6 q | r

✏️ Circle.

1 question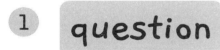

2 roof

3 quiz

4 rainbow

Match and trace.

1 ●   ● quiet

2  ●   ● quiz

3 ●   ● rainbow

4 ●   ● roof

ABC 🖊 Read and write.

 All are red here.

 Red robot and red quilt.

 That is a red roof.

 Look! That is a red rainbow!

s · t

✏️ **Say and write.**

sun

sky

sock

sun

sky

sock

tent

tiger

turtle

tent

tiger

turtle

✶☽☆ **Match.**

s

t

✏️ **Circle.**

1 turtle

2 sun

3 sky

4 tent

✰✕ Match and trace.

1   •   • tiger

2   •   • sun

3  •   • tent

4   •   • sock

ABC✏ Read and write.

 A turtle is in the sea.

 The sun is in the sky.

 The moon and stars are in the sky.

 How beautiful!

25

AB🖊 **Say and write.**

van

vet

vase

van

vet

vase

worm

water

window

worm

water

window

✏️ Circle.

1

v | w

2

v | w

3

v | w

4

v | w

5

v | w

6

v | w

✏️ Circle.

1 van

2 worm

3 window

4 vet

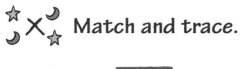 **Match and trace.**

1   • • van

2  • • window

3 • • vase

4   • • water

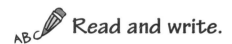 **Read and write.**

 I have a vase.

 I have a window.

 I have a worm.

 What am I? A room, my room!

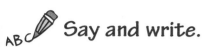

Unit 10 y · z

ABC ✎ Say and write.

yak

yawn

yellow

yak

yawn

yellow

zero

zipper

zigzag

zero

zipper

zigzag

 Match.

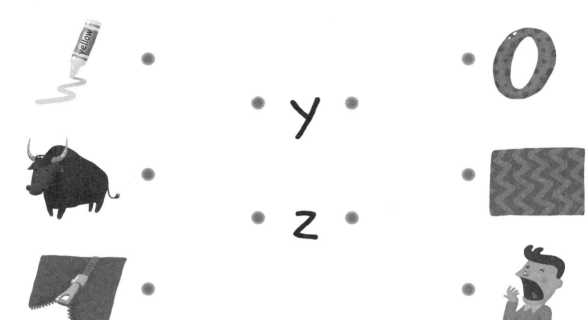

Y

Z

✏️ Circle.

1 zipper

2 yak

3 zigzag

4 yawn

⭐✕🌙 Match and trace.

1  •   • zero

2 •   • yak

3 •   • zigzag

4 🐂 •   • yellow

ABC✏️ Read and write.

 What's that?

 It's a yellow zigzag.

 It's a yellow zipper.

 It's a yak.

Memo